MODERN ROLE MODELS

Yao Ming

Travis Clark

Mason Crest Publishers

Produced by OTTN Publishing in association with
21st Century Publishing and Communications, Inc.

MASON CREST PUBLISHERS INC.
370 Reed Road
Broomall, Pennsylvania 19008
(866) MCP-BOOK (toll free)
www.masoncrest.com

Printed in the United States of America.

First Printing

9 8 7 6 5 4 3 2 1

Library of Congress Cataloging-in-Publication Data

Clark, Travis, 1985–
    Yao Ming / by Travis Clark.
      p. cm. — (Modern role models)
    Includes bibliographical references.
    ISBN-13: 978-1-4222-0484-9 (hardcover) — ISBN-13: 978-1-4222-0772-7 (pbk.)
    ISBN-10: 1-4222-0484-7 (hardcover)
    1. Yao, Ming, 1980–   —Juvenile literature. 2. Basketball players—China—Biography—
Juvenile literature.   I. Title.
    GV884.Y36C563 2009
    796.323092—dc22
    [B]   2008020409

Publisher's note:
All quotations in this book come from original sources, and contain the spelling
and grammatical inconsistencies of the original text.

CROSS-CURRENTS

In the ebb and flow of the currents of life we are each influenced
by many people, places, and events that we directly experience
or have learned about. Throughout the chapters of this book you
will come across **CROSS-CURRENTS** reference boxes. These
boxes direct you to a **CROSS-CURRENTS** section in the back
of the book that contains fascinating and informative sidebars
and related pictures. Go on. ▶▶

CONTENTS

THE
YEAR
OF THE
YAO

From China to the NBA.
From hero to underdog.
The phenomenal journey of Yao Ming.

A poster for the 2004 film *The Year of the Yao*, directed by Adam Del Deo and James D. Stern. The documentary chronicled Yao Ming's rookie season in the National Basketball Association, showing how he fared on the court, how he adapted to life in the United States, and how basketball fans embraced the big man from China.

History Is Made

ON JUNE 26, 2002, YAO MING MADE HISTORY. That day, the Houston Rockets made Yao the number one overall selection in the **National Basketball Association** (NBA) draft. For the first time ever, the NBA's top draft pick had gone for a player who wasn't an American or had never played on an American high school or college basketball team.

➤ THE WAIT IS OVER ➤

At the time the 2002 NBA draft was taking place in New York City, Yao was half a world away, in his hometown of Shanghai, China. As a player for the Shanghai Sharks, he had dominated the domestic league in China over the past season. The year had culminated with his team winning the **Chinese Basketball Association** (CBA)

CROSS-CURRENTS

To learn how other top draft picks have fared, check out "A Sampling of Number One Picks in the NBA Draft." Go to page 50. ▶▶

championship in April of 2002. But playing in the NBA had been a goal of Yao's for several years. In an interview conducted after the draft on NBA.com, he gave some of his reasons:

> **"I want to go [to] the NBA to play a better game because the NBA has the best players in the world. So my purpose in going to the NBA is to play against the best. I think to play in the NBA my target is to win."**

Before the draft, in a series of negotiations with the Sharks, Yao's representatives had secured his release to make him eligible.

But even though he had been the number one draft choice in June 2002, Yao wasn't officially in the NBA just yet. The sticking point was an issue with his contract. While he had been given permission to enter the draft, his contract with the Sharks lasted until December 2002. Final negotiations securing release from his team in Shanghai would continue even after he was selected by the Rockets. On top of that, Chinese basketball officials were hesitant to let Yao live in the United States. They wanted to make sure he would return to China every year and continue to play for the national team after each NBA season. If the details couldn't be resolved to the satisfaction of the Chinese, Houston's number one pick would end up being wasted on a player who dreamed of competing in the NBA but whose country barred him from following that dream.

➤ TEAM YAO ➤

Fortunately, some very capable people wanted to help Yao realize his dream. These people—part of a group that would later be dubbed "Team Yao"—were determined to work out all the logistical difficulties that stood in the way of bringing the Chinese phenom to the United States. The group included Yao's **agent**, Bill Duffy; Erik Zhang, a distant relative of Yao's who lived in Wisconsin; and the assistant dean of the University of Chicago Graduate School of Business, John Huizinga. All three men worked overtime, traveling back and forth between China and the United States. They acted as intermediaries between Chinese

CROSS-CURRENTS

If you'd like to learn about some of the people who helped Yao Ming reach the NBA, read "Meet Team Yao." Go to page 52. ▶▶

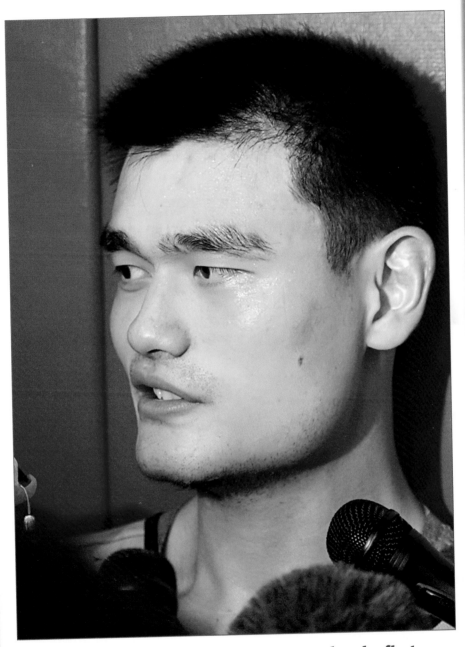

Yao Ming speaks to the media. In 2002, when he first arrived in the United States as the number one draft pick of the Houston Rockets, Yao's English was very limited. He used a translator to help him communicate with sportswriters—as well as with his coaches and teammates.

basketball officials and the NBA, floating proposals and conducting difficult negotiations.

Despite the serious obstacles, the team of Huizinga, Zhang, and Duffy managed to reach an agreement with both the CBA and the Shanghai Sharks before the start of the NBA preseason. The CBA was assured that Yao would continue to represent China on the national level, and the Sharks were well paid to release their star player. By late October of 2002, Yao was officially a member of the Houston Rockets. He was now ready to take on the challenge of competing against the best basketball players in the world.

Accompanied by Chinese officials, Yao walks toward an airport gate to board a flight from China to the United States. "I know there will be a lot of difficulties in front of me," the Chinese star said of his transition to the NBA, "but I'm confident I will learn from the NBA and improve myself."

⟫ NEW COUNTRY, NEW CHALLENGES ⟪

Once he was drafted, Yao had to prepare for his new career in a new country with a vastly different **culture** from his own. He had traveled to the United States before, but he had never experienced anything like this. He was far from **fluent** in English. In fact, he knew only a few words. He would need to use an interpreter throughout most of his first season.

But the biggest challenge Yao faced would no doubt come from playing in the new league. He was transferring from a league that he was used to dominating—he averaged 32 points and 20 rebounds per game during his last season in the CBA—into a league where he would be far from the best basketball player. In the NBA, the game is much faster, and the players are far more skilled and athletic.

But these challenges were what had made Yao want to come to the NBA in the first place, as he told an interviewer on the day he was drafted. Through a translator, Yao said:

> **❝This is now a new start in my basketball life. This is a new league in front of me for me to play, so it will be a new challenge for me. I know there will be a lot of difficulties in front of me, but I'm confident that I will learn from the NBA and improve myself and improve Chinese basketball in the future.❞**

Yao had already made history by being the first player with no connection to American basketball selected with the first overall pick in the NBA draft. But the rest of his story was yet to be written. Would he live up to the hype as China's best basketball player? Or would he follow in the footsteps of some other highly touted number one picks whose pro careers never got off the ground?

Yao brings a special intensity to basketball. A fierce competitor and tireless student of the game, he is driven to be the best. His parents were both excellent players, and Yao was always quite big for his age. Nevertheless, Yao didn't take to basketball right away. At age 12, however, he was sent to a special government-sponsored sports school.

Birth of a Giant

BASKETBALL SEEMED TO BE IN YAO MING'S GENES.
His parents, Yao Zhi Yuan and Fang Fengdi, were both high-level players in China. And they were both tall. Yao's father stood at about 6'8", his mother at about 6'1". With that pedigree, Yao might have been expected to take to basketball from an early age.

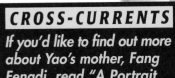

CROSS-CURRENTS
If you'd like to find out more about Yao's mother, Fang Fengdi, read "A Portrait of the Athlete's Mother." Go to page 52.

He did not. That is at least partly because Yao Zhi Yuan and Fang Fengdi didn't want their son to play the game. At the time of their marriage in 1977, the couple were both veterans of China's national basketball program—Fang had even led the Chinese women's team to victory in the 1976 Asian Championships. But when Yao was born in Shanghai on October 26, 1980, his parents' playing days were behind them. The Chinese government had assigned Yao Zhi Yuan to work at a factory, while his wife was placed at a sports and recreation center. Both had sacrificed a large portion of their youth training for basketball. Neither wanted that future for their son.

⟫ NO HOOP DREAMS ⟪

During Yao's early childhood years, it seemed his parents had nothing to worry about on that count. He was always tall for his age—by the time he entered first grade, Yao stood at 4'9", nearly a foot taller than most of his classmates. But, as his biographer C. F. Xiao notes, the tall boy had no passion for basketball:

> **"Yao Ming, Yao Ming's parents, and his teachers and coaches, as well as his companions at that time, all say that at first he didn't like basketball at all, and that during those years basketball was just another game to him. "**

Eventually, however, Yao's height began to attract the attention of Chinese basketball officials.

⟫ STUDENT OF THE GAME ⟪

In China, it is common policy to identify children who show extraordinary athletic promise, and to send these children to specialized government-funded schools, where they receive intensive training. When Yao was 12 years old, he began to train at the Xu Jia Hui District Youth Sports School. This is where he first played basketball on a regular basis. Recognizing Yao's enormous potential, the school requested a special government **grant** for his training alone.

In 1994, when Yao was 14, he was picked to join the Shanghai youth team. By this time his height topped 6'7". A local newspaper described him as "a crane towering over a flock of chickens." While playing on the Shanghai youth team, Yao met Liu Wei, a point guard who soon became one of his best friends—and still is to this day.

CROSS-CURRENTS

Shanghai, Yao's hometown, is China's most populous city. To learn more about this enormous metropolis, see "Shanghai." Go to page 53. ▶▶

⟫ PLAYING WITH THE SHARKS ⟪

At age 16, Yao stood almost 7'2" tall. He had worked his way onto the youth team of the

Shanghai Sharks, a Chinese Basketball Association club. The CBA, established in 1995, was a professional league (although the Chinese government exercised considerable control over how it was run). The CBA's teams included the best basketball talent in China.

As a member of the Sharks' youth team, Yao was still one step away from the highest level of Chinese competitive basketball. But as he traveled all over the country to play, Yao impressed fans and coaches alike. It seemed only a matter of time before this young giant was ready to play in the CBA.

Chinese players warm up before a game. In 1995 the Chinese Basketball Association (CBA), the country's premier professional league, was established. By the following year, 16-year-old Yao Ming—who already stood 7'2" tall—had won a spot on the youth team of the CBA's Shanghai Sharks. In 1997 he appeared in his first CBA game.

Shortly before his 17th birthday, in fact, Yao did make his first appearance with the Shanghai Sharks. On October 13, 1997, the Sharks played the team from Shangdong. Six minutes into the game, Yao debuted. Despite his height, he struggled to keep up with the older, more experienced players. At this point, Yao could not match their skill and agility.

With the higher level of competition, however, Yao's game steadily improved. And as he developed, the Sharks—a seventh-place team in 1997—also began to improve.

⇒ INTERNATIONAL EXPERIENCE ⇐

Around the time he started playing at the highest levels of Chinese basketball, Yao traveled overseas and got a taste of international competition. In June 1997 he took his first trip outside China, attending a basketball camp in France. There Yao—one of only three Chinese players at the camp—played against talented young athletes from all over the world.

A year after that, Yao traveled to the United States with his friend Liu Wei. They played with an **Amateur Athletic Union** (AAU) team that toured the country. As a result of his play on the AAU team, Yao attracted enough attention to be hired as a counselor at a camp run by NBA legend Michael Jordan. This experience gave him a chance to practice against players who were working to be drafted into the NBA.

By 1998 basketball insiders had begun to take notice of Yao Ming. In July of that year sportswriter Robin Miller wrote about Yao in an article for the *Indianapolis Star*:

> **❝**He's 7 feet 5 inches tall, weighs 252 pounds, has an arm span of 9 feet 3 inches, and can make 15-foot jump shots with agility; he can also turn and attack beneath the basketball.**❞**

Soon he would get to display his talent on a much larger stage.

⇒ SYDNEY OLYMPICS ⇐

In 1999 China's national men's basketball team defeated defending champion South Korea to win the title at the Asian Championships. This qualified the Chinese team to compete at the 2000 Summer Olympics, held in Sydney, Australia.

Basketball legend Michael Jordan poses with rising star Yao Ming during the NBA's 2003 All-Star Weekend in Atlanta, Georgia. The two had first met five years before, when Yao worked as a counselor at Jordan's basketball camp. Jordan, arguably basketball's greatest player of all time, retired after the 2002–2003 NBA season.

In the first round, China drew the powerhouse U.S. team, which was loaded with NBA stars such as Vince Carter, Kevin Garnett, Jason Kidd, and Alonzo Mourning. The Americans—who went on to win the gold medal at Sydney—easily dispatched the Chinese team, 119-72. Although his team lost the game by 47 points, Yao had made his presence felt. Despite fouling out early in the second half, he scored 5 points, grabbed 3 rebounds, and blocked several shots.

Before Yao took the NBA by storm in 2002, another Chinese big man had tried his luck on basketball's premier stage. Wang Zhizhi, a 7'1" center for the perennial CBA champion Bayi Rockets, was drafted by the Dallas Mavericks in 1999. He played five lackluster seasons in the NBA—with Dallas, the Los Angeles Clippers, and the Miami Heat—before returning to China in 2005.

Mourning, the American center, was especially impressed by the play of his Chinese counterpart:

> **"He is really talented. Seldom do you have some-body like him who is tall and fast at the same time; he's a genius. He's only 20, and he can pass and also shoot. But he has to work on his strength."**

Yao gained confidence as a result of his experiences in Sydney. He realized that he could compete with NBA stars—and he started dreaming of playing in the NBA.

The Olympics also helped bring about a change in Yao's personal life. For several years he had been trying, without success, to attract the attention of Li Ye, a member of China's national women's basketball team. After the Olympics, Yao gave some of his team pins to Li, and the two began to date.

⇒ STRIVING FOR THE **NBA** ⇐

Before realizing his dream of playing in the NBA, Yao wanted to bring a championship to Shanghai. He came close in 2000 and 2001, as his team finished second to the Bayi Rockets in back-to-back seasons. It wasn't until after Bayi star Wang Zhizhi left for the NBA that Yao was able to achieve his goal. At the end of the 2001–2002 season, he led the Sharks to their first-ever CBA title. With that goal attained, Yao believed, it was time to push for the NBA.

But talent alone wouldn't land Yao on the roster of a NBA team. First he would have to get the Chinese Basketball Association to release him. Then he would have to agree to contract terms with the NBA team that drafted him. Yao needed an agent to negotiate for him. In the end, it was not a single agent, but several people—"Team Yao"—who took up Yao's cause. Through a series of negotiations they helped Yao become eligible for the draft in which the Houston Rockets made him the first overall pick.

CROSS-CURRENTS

Yao is not the only Chinese to have played professionally in America. Others are profiled in "Chinese Players in the NBA."
Go to page 54. ▶▶

The moment the Houston Rockets made him the first overall pick in the 2002 draft, Yao Ming entered the limelight. The pressure to perform well—which all number one picks experience—was intensified by Yao's unique circumstances. As his country took an increasingly prominent role on the world stage, Yao became a symbol of Chinese pride.

The Start of Something New

AFTER BEING DRAFTED BY THE HOUSTON ROCKETS, Yao couldn't wait to go to the United States and begin his NBA career. He even learned a few words in English to introduce himself to Rockets fans. "I am very happy to join the Houston Rockets," he told an interviewer on NBA.com. "Hi, Houston, I'm coming."

However, there was still work to be done, as Yao hadn't officially been released from his team in Shanghai. It wasn't at all certain that he would be able to join the Rockets by the start of the NBA season in October. The Chinese Basketball Association wanted some guarantees that Yao wouldn't abandon China's national team during international competitions. In addition, Yao's old team, the Shanghai Sharks, insisted on being paid for giving up their star player.

CROSS-CURRENTS

"Differences Between Chinese and U.S. Basketball" explains how big-time hoops varies in the two societies. *Go to page 55.* ▶▶

These hurdles were finally cleared almost four months after the draft. Yao would indeed be playing for the Houston Rockets during the 2002–2003 NBA season.

⇛ ALL KINDS OF PRESSURE ⇚

The move to Houston, Texas, would signal a big change in Yao's life. For the first time, he was going to live in a city other than Shanghai. In addition to his unfamiliarity with the physical surroundings, Yao would have to make his way in a culture that was very different from the one in which he had grown up. Plus, he could barely speak

Media sensation: Surrounded by a throng of reporters, Yao takes time to autograph a basketball for a young fan shortly after his arrival in Houston. The man standing to Yao's right and holding a book is Colin Pine. He would serve as Yao's full-time translator as the big man adjusted to life in the United States.

the language. To help ease the transition, Yao's mother and father planned to live with him in Houston.

But the challenge of adapting to life in a foreign country wasn't the only hurdle Yao faced. On the basketball court, he would bear the pressure of having been selected first overall in the NBA draft. Expectations for number one draft picks are always incredibly high. Fans often believe these players should make an immediate impact. Coaches and general managers, too, may be anxious to see their investment pay quick dividends.

Yao had an additional kind of pressure, and it was one that most young players from the United States probably couldn't even understand. Yao wasn't simply following his own dreams to succeed in the NBA. He also carried the hopes of his countrymen, who were eager to see one of their own succeed on the world stage. Many of China's 1.3 billion people would be following Yao's every move. If he flopped in the NBA, a lot of people would be enormously disappointed. But Yao was determined to prove himself to everyone—American fans, his fellow Chinese, his coaches, his teammates.

⟫ A Big Momma's Boy ⟪

Yao's mother arrived in Houston in early October of 2002. She bought a house for him in the Houston suburbs. Later, after her son had arrived, she helped him settle in. Throughout his rookie season, Fang lived with her son, cooking and cleaning for him. Yao's father joined his wife and son after the season had begun. Needless to say, these living arrangements were a bit unusual among NBA players. But having his parents with him helped Yao adjust to his new life.

Other arrangements were made to help Yao communicate. He had visited the United States briefly before, but his English was very limited. He couldn't speak or understand enough words to field reporters' postgame questions. A translator had to be hired. More than 400 people applied for the job. Erik Zhang, a cousin of Yao's and one of the key members of "Team Yao," interviewed the final candidates. Eventually he and Yao chose a young man named Colin Pine, who had done translation work for the U.S. State Department. Pine would travel everywhere with the Rockets, and he even moved in with Yao and his parents. Pine served as Yao's translator for his first two seasons in the NBA.

Rookie Yao Ming absorbs some basketball lessons from his Houston Rockets teammate Kelvin Cato, a five-year veteran. As always, Colin Pine is present to translate. At the end of his first season, Yao would credit Cato, a journeyman center, for helping him adjust to playing center in the NBA.

⇒ NEW TEAMMATES, NEW SEASON ⇐

The Rockets' 2002–2003 season opened on October 30 with an away game at Indianapolis. As Yao had arrived in the United States a mere 10 days earlier, he didn't have much time to get used to playing with his new teammates, or to figure out the system of his new coach, Rudy Tomjanovich. In addition, he was very anxious about performing well. As he recalled in *Yao Ming: A Life in Two Worlds*:

> **❝I felt especially nervous before my first regular-season game in the NBA, of course, but even more so because it was in Indianapolis. Yes I'd played**

there in the World Championships, but the arena in Indianapolis is very big, and there weren't a lot of people there for the championships. It was like a different place for my first Rockets game: lots of people, lots of media, lots of noise.**"**

Perhaps all this explains Yao's subpar performance in his NBA debut. He simply didn't play well, as Yao himself acknowledged:

"I still don't know what happened to me in that first game against the Pacers. . . . I never woke up. I played only eleven minutes and missed the only

Yao can't seem to get his hands on a rebound during action from his rookie season. Yao's NBA career got off to a shaky start. But the Chinese big man soon silenced critics such as Charles Barkley, whose prediction that Yao wouldn't score 19 points in a game all season was proved wrong only a month into the 2002–2003 campaign.

shot I took. . . . I thought the Rockets might just send me back to China the next day. **"**

Yao didn't have a long time to beat himself up over a poor debut, however. The Rockets' next game was only two nights later. He knew that he had to shake off his poor performance and move on. It was in his second game that he scored his first basket in the NBA.

≫ A ROLLER-COASTER ROOKIE SEASON ≪

As Yao's first season progressed, he improved steadily. He learned how to run the plays Tomjanovich designed, and he adjusted to the NBA's quicker pace of play. Tomjanovich began to figure out how to use Yao's strengths to best suit his offense. Houston's star point guard at the time, Steve Francis, had been the cornerstone of the team before Yao's arrival. Now, a lot of the attention had switched to the tall Chinese center. Francis did a great deal to integrate Yao into the team's offense, and off the court he and all the other Rockets played a crucial role in helping Yao adjust to his new surroundings.

Yet even with the support of his teammates and his parents, Yao—like most rookies—had his ups and downs. In one game, he would record a double-double, scoring 10 or more points and pulling down 10 or more rebounds. But in the next game, he might have almost no impact. Such inconsistency is not at all unusual for a young player in the NBA, and it often goes largely unnoticed. But Yao's status as a number one overall draft pick—along with his Chinese nationality—ensured that the spotlight was always on him. His roller-coaster play, though it was just part of his development as an NBA player, was constantly scrutinized.

≫ CHINESE SIDESHOW ≪

After bringing Yao off the bench in the first 10 games, Tomjanovich put the Chinese center in his starting lineup. Yao would remain a starter for the rest of the season.

Yao brought a strong, intimidating inside presence to the Rockets. He also brought a great deal of media attention. Chinese reporters followed the team around the United States, reporting back to China on the progress of the country's most famous athlete.

In November 2002, voting for the NBA All-Star Game began. Each year, fans get to vote for the five players who start for each conference.

Yao was one of the biggest stories in the NBA during the 2002–2003 season. These giant reproductions of *Sports Illustrated* covers—from the magazine's preseason- and midseason-report issues—adorn a street in Shanghai, where residents of Yao's hometown could take pride in the accomplishments of the city's favorite son.

After the starters are selected, coaches throughout the league are polled to determine the other seven players on each side. Yao's name was on the ballot, and—to the surprise of many basketball insiders—the rookie was voted the Western Conference's starting center.

While some experts argued that Yao didn't deserve to make the All-Star Game—and certainly didn't deserve to start over Shaquille O'Neal—his play at around the halfway point of the season was strong. Despite his All-Star

CROSS-CURRENTS

To read about how Yao fared in his first matchups with Shaquille O'Neal, see "Shaq vs. Yao: Battle of the Twin Towers" on page 56. ▶▶

selection, he remained humble and self-effacing, as his recollections in *Yao Ming: A Life in Two Worlds* attest:

> **"Maybe not all NBA players feel this way, but I think of all the players who came into the league with me as my brothers. That's why, on All-Star**

Yao Ming, the Western Conference's starting center, slams over his Eastern Conference counterpart, Ben Wallace of the Detroit Pistons, during the All-Star Game, February 9, 2003. The dunk provided Yao's only points of the game. Nevertheless, the West won the double-overtime contest by a score of 155-145.

Weekend, I wanted to sit on the West team bench during the Rookie Game, even though I couldn't play because I was in the All-Star Game. I just wanted to be with my brothers. **"**

❧ FINISHING STRONG ❦

After the All-Star Game, Yao's first season was more than halfway over. But ahead stretched some difficult months. The NBA season is an exhausting grind. Eighty-two games running up and down the hardwood floor, jumping, bumping, and being fouled by big, strong players, takes a toll on the body. By the final weeks of the season, almost every NBA player is worn down physically and has some nagging pains. Yao was particularly tired. He had spent the previous summer working out and playing with the Chinese national team. He had begun the NBA season without benefit of a break during which to rest and rebuild his strength. And he wasn't going to get a chance to rest anytime soon. Houston was in the hunt for a playoff berth in the Western Conference.

Yao, despite his fatigue, ended up playing in all 82 games in his rookie season. Unfortunately, the Rockets missed the playoffs by a single game. A major distraction had confronted the team during the stretch drive. In March, Rudy Tomjanovich announced that he was taking a leave of absence from coaching. Tomjanovich had been diagnosed with bladder cancer.

Although the season ended on a bit of a sour note, Yao could look back on his first NBA year with satisfaction. He had averaged 13.5 points and 8.2 rebounds per game. And, while many NBA big men have trouble at the foul line, Yao had made an impressive 81 percent of his free throws.

Yao finished second in the voting for NBA Rookie of the Year. Amare Stoudemire of the Phoenix Suns garnered that honor.

At the end of the season, an exhausted Yao left Houston for Shanghai. As part of his agreement to play in the NBA, Yao was required to return to China every year, mostly to train with the Chinese national team. He was determined to hone his game further during the NBA off-season.

Yao acknowledges the cheering crowd after a home-court victory. Houston Rockets fans were quick to embrace the big man—both for his hardworking style of play and for his good-natured, self-effacing personality off the court. Yao also became a fan favorite at other cities around the league.

A Growing Star

THE ROCKETS HAD HEARD MANY DOUBTERS WHEN they drafted Yao number one overall. But after a year of exposure in the NBA, Yao had clearly shown that he was a fine basketball player as well as a decent human being. As his career progressed, Yao would continue to demonstrate his strength both on and off the court.

⇛ FIGHTING SARS ⇚

When Yao returned to China after his first NBA season, the country was in the midst of a public health panic. A mysterious disease dubbed **severe acute respiratory syndrome (SARS)** had broken out.

Yao decided to help raise money to fight SARS. On May 11, 2003—less than a month after the end of his NBA season—Yao hosted the first **telethon** in China's history. His effort was a testament to his character, as an article in *BusinessWeek* noted:

"The three-hour show, *Stars vs. SARS*, raised more than $300,000 to fight the epidemic . . . Yao's return home and his hosting of the telethon reveal a generosity that is matched by a humility unusual in a sports star.**"**

⟫ SECOND SEASON ⟪

While Yao was in China during the off-season, the Houston Rockets were mapping out their future. The team hired a new coach, Jeff Van Gundy, formerly head coach of the New York Knicks.

Van Gundy decided to make Yao—rather than Steve Francis—the focus of the team's offense. He also expected his 7'6" center to anchor the defense. This would put a lot of additional pressure on Yao, but the big man responded. Starting all 82 games, Yao averaged 17.5 points and 9 rebounds per game. He also blocked almost 2 shots per game. For the second year in a row, Yao was selected as a starter on the Western Conference's All-Star team.

Over the course of Yao's second NBA season, many of his Houston teammates noticed how an improving Yao improved the entire team. In an interview with *Basketball Digest* writer Brett Ballantini, guard Steve Francis talked about Yao's progress:

"Yao's a lot better adjusted now. He has a year under his belt. He knows what the NBA is like and has a sense of his place in the league. He still has a lot to learn recognizing offenses and defenses, but he's getting it. There's no way not to be optimistic about how things are going with him and the team.**"**

The combination of Yao, Francis, and shooting guard Cuttino Mobley propelled the Rockets to a 45-37 season and a playoff berth. However, Houston ran into the Los Angeles Lakers in the first round of the playoffs, and L.A. took the series, 4-1.

⟫ HONORED BY HIS COUNTRY ⟪

After the 2004 playoffs, the Rockets made a blockbuster trade. Houston sent Francis, Mobley, and Kelvin Cato to the Orlando Magic in exchange for Tracy McGrady, Juwan Howard, and two other players.

Jeff Van Gundy, hired after the 2002–2003 season to replace Rudy Tomjanovich as Houston's head coach, talks to his players during a break in the action of a December 2004 game at Cleveland. The acquisition of high-scoring guard Tracy McGrady, along with Yao's continued development, helped propel the Rockets to a 54-35 finish for the 2004–2005 season.

But Yao had little time to dwell on his next NBA season. He had received a great honor from his country. On August 13, 2004, he carried the flag of China during the opening ceremonies of the Summer Olympics, which were held in Athens, Greece.

Yao also represented his country during the basketball competition. The Chinese national team finished eighth overall.

⇒ SLOW ADJUSTMENT ⇐

When he reported to training camp for the start of his third NBA season, Yao had new teammates to adjust to on the court. With Steve Francis gone, newly acquired guard/forward Tracy McGrady was expected to pick up much of the offensive slack. T-Mac had proven he could score—over the previous two seasons, he had averaged 32 and 28 points per game. Yet he had also gained a reputation as a ball hog and was widely regarded as a difficult teammate. Many basketball insiders wondered whether Yao and T-Mac would get along.

Yao Ming is second from right in this poster for the NBA's 2005 All-Star Game, held February 20 in Denver. Yao, tapped for his third consecutive All-Star start, scored 11 points and pulled down 8 rebounds in 22 minutes of play. But the East won the game, 125-115, on the strength of 15 points from MVP Allen Iverson (fourth from left).

Before the start of the season, Yao got the chance to show his teammates a bit of his country. In October 2004, the Rockets played preseason games against the Sacramento Kings in Shanghai and Beijing. This marked the first time that NBA games of any kind were played in China.

Once the regular season got under way, the Rockets struggled. After the first month of the season, Houston's record stood at a lackluster 6-11. Yao and McGrady seemed to have little on-court chemistry.

CROSS-CURRENTS
"China Games and the NBA-China Relationship" looks at the history of American professional basketball teams playing in China. Go to page 57.

By January 2005, however, the team started to right itself as McGrady and Yao began to play well together. There was still time to make a push for the playoffs.

In the meantime, basketball fans selected Yao as an All-Star starter for the third consecutive season. His vote total of 2,558,278 set a record.

Yao in his third NBA season wasn't just wildly popular. His offensive numbers were rock solid. He averaged 18.4 points, 8.5 rebounds, and 2.0 blocked shots per game.

ANOTHER EARLY EXIT

Behind the play of Yao and T-Mac, the Rockets finished with a regular-season mark of 51-31. That was Houston's best record in 10 years, and it was good enough for the fifth spot overall in the Western Conference.

In the first round of the playoffs, the Rockets faced in-state rivals the Dallas Mavericks. Houston appeared to put a stranglehold on the series by winning the first two games on the Mavericks' home court. McGrady was the hero of Game 1, scoring 34 points to pace Houston to a 98-86 victory. Yao chipped in with 11 points and 8 rebounds. In the next meeting, a thrilling game that Houston won 113-111, Yao was nothing short of sensational. He shot a sizzling 13 of 14 from the field and was a perfect 7 for 7 from the foul line en route to a game-high 33 points. Coming home with a 2-0 series advantage, the Rockets seemed poised to advance.

But the Mavericks won the next two contests on Houston's home court, then followed up with another victory in Dallas. The Rockets found themselves facing elimination at home in Game 6. Offensive fireworks from Tracy McGrady prevented that from happening. T-Mac scored 37 points to lead Houston to a 101-83 spanking of Dallas.

The series would come down to a decisive seventh game on the Mavericks' home court. Yao did his part, scoring 33 points and grabbing 10 rebounds; McGrady added 27 points. But otherwise it was all Dallas, which administered a 116-76 beating of the Rockets. Yao and his teammates had suffered another first-round exit from the playoffs.

⇒ FIGHTING OFF INJURY ⇐

Despite their playoff disappointment, the Rockets entered the 2005–2006 season with considerable optimism. T-Mac and Yao had turned into a dynamic scoring duo, and they were surrounded by a solid cast of supporting players.

From the outset, however, the Rockets faced setbacks. McGrady suffered a back injury during the first month of the regular season. After that, Houston went into a tailspin, losing seven games in a row at the end of November. In December, soon after T-Mac returned to the lineup, Yao was lost to injury. A severe infection in his big toe forced him to have surgery. He missed several weeks of the season.

Still, the situation turned out for the best. Yao had been playing with an infected toe for years—since his days with the Shanghai Sharks of the CBA, as a matter of fact. The Sharks didn't have the medical personnel to treat the condition, however. After receiving treatment in the United States, Yao noticed a dramatic improvement, as he told ESPN's Ric Bucher:

> **"You wouldn't believe the difference. Imagine playing with a rock in your shoe and not on the bottom, but on the top. Every game, every day. I got used to it, and sometimes it was worse than other times. But it feels so good now."**

⇒ YAO UNLEASHED ⇐

After his return to the lineup and another appearance at the All-Star Game, Yao went on an extended tear. Over the course of the final 25 games, he averaged 25.7 points and 11.6 rebounds per game. But his individual heroics weren't enough to save Houston from a dismal 34-48 record and a last-place finish in the Southwest Division. Needless to say, the team missed the playoffs.

Despite his team's poor performance, Yao found himself being showered with praise. His numbers for the entire season—more than

As Yao's teammate Juwan Howard looks on, Dwyane Wade of the Miami Heat tries to get around the man nicknamed "the Great Wall of China" in a 2005 game in Houston. At 7'6" tall and with his huge arm span, Yao is a force near the basket—at the defensive and offensive ends of the floor.

Yao drives around New York Knicks center Eddy Curry during a game at Madison Square Garden in New York, February 5, 2006. The Rockets won the game but suffered through a difficult season, finishing in last place in the Southwest Division. Yao's season ended prematurely, when he broke his foot in April.

20 points and 10 rebounds per game—placed him among the NBA's elite centers. Yao had become the dominating player the Rockets had been hoping for when they drafted him.

⟫ AGONY OF THE FEET ⟪

Although he had come into his own as an NBA big man, the 2005–2006 season didn't end well for Yao. On April 10, 2006, he broke his foot in a game against the Utah Jazz. Yao had a history of foot problems: twice before, in Shanghai, he had broken his foot.

This break would have plenty of time to heal before the 2006–2007 NBA season, which wasn't scheduled to get under way until October. But Yao desperately wanted to take to the court before then. Over the summer, the World Championships were being held in Japan, and Yao wanted to play for China's national team. In a *Houston Chronicle* article, he spoke of his desire to represent his country:

> **"The final goal before I came to the NBA was to play for the national team and for my country in the Olympics. Now that I am in the NBA, that is still a very important goal for me. . . . If you play for the national team and they didn't pay or they didn't have fans and if they even put me on the bench like a role player—I wouldn't care because it is an honor to play for my country."**

For a while, it appeared that Yao's injury could prevent him from playing. But as the off-season progressed, his foot healed well enough that he could take part in the World Championships. Yao led all scorers with 25.3 points per game, though China finished the tournament in 15th place overall.

Yao's stature had grown immensely since his arrival in the NBA four short years earlier. Then, many people had doubted that he had the athleticism to play with the NBA's best. Now, he was widely viewed as one of the top big men in the league. Since joining the Rockets, Yao had been voted to the All-Star Game every year. And his best was yet to come.

A tourist poses with a wax figure of Yao Ming, Shanghai, China. Since entering the NBA in 2002, Yao has become one of the most recognized athletes in the world. Although he tries to maintain some privacy in his personal life, Yao has used his international celebrity to promote a variety of good causes.

Larger Than Life

BY 2006 FEW BASKETBALL FANS HAD NOT HEARD of Yao Ming. In fact, the 7'6" Chinese basketball star had become one of the most recognized athletes in the entire world. And he was celebrated not just for his exploits on the court but also for his humanitarian work off the court.

➤ EXCITEMENT FOR A NEW SEASON ◄

After his strong performance at the 2006 World Championships, Yao was primed to take the NBA by storm. On the eve of the 2006–2007 season, forward Shane Battier said of his Chinese teammate:

> **"He's arguably the top center in the game today. Last year, he reached a point he was truly, truly dominant. I think it was the dominance people were waiting to see. Unfortunately, he got hurt and was not able to carry that dominance to finish the season."**

Pop culture icon: an animated Yao Ming, along with football's Warren Sapp and Tom Brady, fellow NBA star LeBron James, and figure skater Michelle Kwan, join the feckless Homer on an episode of *The Simpsons*. The episode, "Homer and Ned's Hail Mary Pass," first aired February 7, 2005, after Super Bowl XXIX.

In the early weeks of the season, Yao validated Battier's high opinion of him. In November, the first month of the regular season, Yao averaged 25.7 points and 10.1 rebounds per game. His increasingly dominant play earned the big man NBA Player of the Month honors.

Yao continued to play superbly through the first three weeks of December. Most important, the McGrady-Yao combination was clicking, and the Rockets were off to a flying start.

⟫ ANOTHER INJURY ⟪

Once again, however, a serious injury sidelined the Chinese super-star. In a December 23 game against the Los Angeles Clippers, Yao fractured his right leg. Doctors said he would miss at least six weeks of the season.

But this time, even without Yao in the lineup, the Rockets were able to keep winning. He rested and rehabbed his leg for the next two months—missing 32 games.

Professional basketball can be a rough game, particularly when big men bang one another under the basket. Yao Ming has sustained his share of injuries on the court. Some, such as fractured bones in his leg and feet, have been season ending. Others, like the cut to his right temple shown in this photo, are all in a day's work for an NBA star.

Despite his extended absence from the court, the ever-popular Yao was once again voted to start in the 2007 NBA All-Star Game. His injury prevented him from participating, however.

⇒ RETURN TO THE PLAYOFFS ⇐

It wasn't until the beginning of March 2007 that Yao received medical clearance to play. He picked up right where he had left off in December. Joining McGrady, Yao led the Rockets on a stretch drive that gave the team a final regular-season record of 52-30. Once again the Rockets had made the playoffs. This time their excellent record secured them home-court advantage against their first-round opponent, the Utah Jazz.

Behind Yao's 28 points and 13 rebounds, Houston won the first game, 84-75, on April 21. Two days later McGrady dropped 31 points, and Yao 27, as the Rockets won Game 2 by a score of 98-90.

Utah struck back, winning the next two games on its home court. In each of these games, Yao led all scorers and rebounders, but his Rockets were nevertheless beaten by double-digit margins.

With the teams knotted at two games apiece, the series resumed in Houston on April 30. Yao and the Rockets recaptured the series lead and pushed Utah to the brink of elimination with a 96-92 win.

But Utah won the next game at home, 94-82, forcing a decisive seventh game in Houston. That game, played on May 5, was a nail-biter. But in the end, the Jazz came out on top, 103-99. Despite scoring 29 points, Yao blamed himself for the season-ending loss, as he had pulled down only six rebounds:

> **"I didn't do my job. I didn't do a very good job of rebounding. Rebound, rebound, rebound. Whatever, long rebound, short rebound—it's my job to rebound. . . . I didn't do my job. "**

There was little time to stew over the loss, however. Yao had a busy summer ahead of him.

⇒ HARDLY A VACATION ⇐

For Yao, the NBA off-season had rarely been restful. He usually spent a great deal of the time training back in China or making appearances for charity. The summer of 2007 turned out to be no less busy.

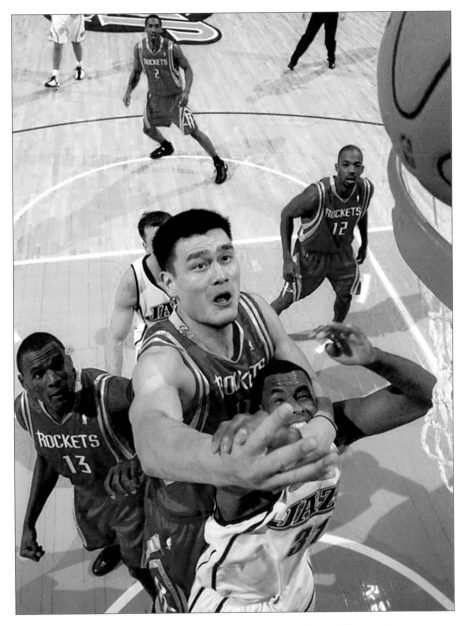

As teammates Kirk Snyder (#13) and Rafer Allston (#12) look on, Yao battles Utah Jazz center Jarron Collins for a rebound during the fourth game of the Rockets' first-round playoff series against Utah, April 28, 2007. The Jazz won the game, 98-85, and went on to take the series, four games to two.

In June, Yao and his girlfriend of eight years, Li Ye, announced they would marry in August.

In addition to planning a wedding, Yao also helped China kick off its countdown to the 2008 Summer Olympics, which were to be hosted by Beijing. With much fanfare, the 400-day countdown to the Olympics began in early July 2007. Chinese officials thought it important to have Yao, the country's most famous athlete, present for the countdown celebration, and he obliged.

Right after that celebration, Yao hopped on a plane to fly back to his hometown of Shanghai. There he took part in the NBA program **Basketball Without Borders**. This was the third year in a row that the program was taking place in China, and the second year in a row that the program was held in Shanghai. From July 6–8, more than 50 Asian basketball players gathered for a three-day **mini-camp** run by current and former NBA stars.

CROSS-CURRENTS

Basketball has become internationally popular. To learn about a global program that teaches basketball skills, read "Basketball Without Borders." Go to page 57. ▶▶

Yao's next big event of the summer was his wedding. Yao and Li Ye, who began dating in 2001, were married on August 6, 2007. The wedding ceremony, held at a hotel in Shanghai, was small and low-key. Only about 70 invited guests were present. Still, many people in China were fascinated by the wedding of their country's most famous celebrity, and the Chinese press was abuzz with breathless reports.

⇒ CHARITY IN CHINA ⇐

While still in China, Yao continued his charitable off-season work. On August 31 it was announced that a team of traveling NBA players would play against Yao and a team of Chinese players. Steve Nash, the point guard for the Phoenix Suns, would lead the NBA team. The proceeds of the two charity games would go to the China Youth Development Foundation. This organization helps fund education for young children in western and central China, where many schools are inadequate.

The two charity games, played in Beijing, became a huge media event, with an estimated 250 million people watching on Chinese television. The games helped raise $2.5 million, enough money to build almost 70 schools in poverty-stricken areas of China.

姚明·纳什
慈善之旅义赛

emma
TICKET 爱玛票务
www.emma.cn
400 707 9999

姚 明	王治郅	史蒂夫·纳 什
易建联	李 楠	卡梅罗·安东尼
刘 炜	孙 悦	德里克·费舍尔
		林德罗·巴博萨

Yao and point guard Steve Nash are featured on this Chinese poster publicizing two exhibition games, played for charity in China during the summer of 2007. The games, which matched a team of NBA stars led by Nash against a team of Chinese stars led by Yao, raised $2.5 million for the construction of schools in impoverished areas of China.

Once the charity games were over, Yao lent his time to another good cause. His hometown of Shanghai was hosting the Special Olympics—games in which athletes with physical and mental handicaps participate. Yao took part in the opening ceremonies and made an appearance on the field during the competition.

Yao pushes aside 6'11" forward Kevin Garnett of the Boston Celtics to slam home a dunk in a game at Boston's FleetCenter, January 2, 2008. Houston lost the game, dropping its record to 15-17. But the team soon caught fire, finishing the season with a record of 55-27. Unfortunately, Yao was diagnosed with a season-ending stress fracture in late February.

At the end of the summer, Yao managed to find time to practice with the Chinese national basketball team. The team was getting ready for the 2008 Olympic Games.

BACK TO THE NBA

With the whirlwind of an off-season complete, it was now time for Yao to prepare for the 2007–2008 NBA season. Houston had made a few moves over the summer. The team had acquired Argentina-born forward Luis Scola. Yao's former teammate Steve Francis, who had been playing for the Orlando Magic, rejoined the Rockets. And Jeff Van Gundy, Houston's head coach, had been fired. He was replaced by veteran coach Rick Adelman, who had previously spent eight seasons at the helm of the Sacramento Kings.

During the preseason, Yao expressed concerns about his understanding of Adelman's system. As he told the *Houston Chronicle* in October, he worried that he—as well as the team—might not be ready for the start of the regular season:

> **I think I need a few more [games]. We of course have new coach, new assistant coaches, new teammates coming in, we need more time for practice, more time for game, to [increase] our chemistry.**

HOUSTON, WE HAVE A PROBLEM

Despite Yao's concerns, the Rockets got off to a fast start when the regular season began. With Yao looking sharp, the team won six of its first seven games.

But, as in seasons past, injuries began to strike. Tracy McGrady missed a handful of games in the early part of the season. The team struggled through December and January, with its record hovering within a few games of .500. But Yao's play was outstanding. He averaged 22 points and more than 10 rebounds per game. His stellar performance earned him a sixth consecutive trip to the All-Star Game.

As January came to a close, Houston's record stood at a mediocre 24-20. Then the team caught fire, reeling off a dozen wins in a row. This, it seemed, might be the year Yao played deep into the postseason, and perhaps even helped his team to a championship. In late February, however, the big man was diagnosed with a stress fracture in his left foot. Yao's season was over.

➤ THE BIGGEST LOSS ➤

The premature end of his NBA season was hard enough to take. But Yao was devastated by the possibility that he wouldn't be able to participate in the Summer Olympics, scheduled to begin in August in his native China. "If I cannot play in the Olympics for my country this time," Yao remarked, "it will be the biggest loss in my career to right now."

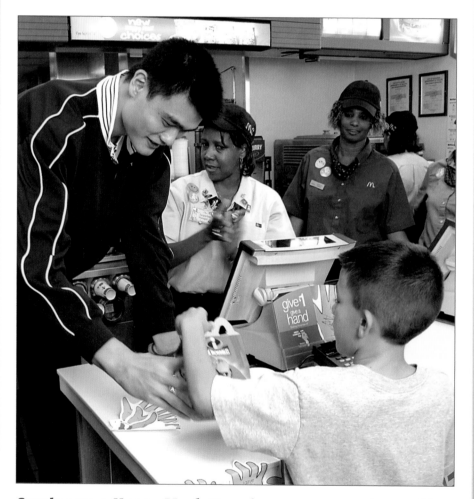

Serving up a Happy Meal: Yao gives a young customer his food at a Houston McDonald's restaurant, November 20, 2007. The basketball superstar lent his time to help publicize World Children's Day, and McDonald's donated a portion of its profits to a variety of charities serving kids.

No one who knew Yao was prepared to say categorically that the big man wouldn't be playing for China in the 2008 Olympics. Yao is a tough competitor. He also carries the enormous expectations of his countrymen. And he faces—as he has long faced—intense pressure from Chinese officials to play on the national team.

Over the years, this pressure has been the source of friction between the Rockets and China. Every off-season, Yao dutifully returns to his native land to train with the Chinese national team. It isn't unreasonable to suggest that the wear and tear of playing almost year-round has contributed to Yao's injury problems.

⇒ BIG MAN WITH A BIG HEART ⇐

Because he remains in the eye of both the Chinese and the U.S. media, Yao Ming has grown into one of the world's biggest celebrities. His height makes it nearly impossible for him to go anywhere without being noticed. But the size of his heart matches, if not outstrips, his physical size. Countless times Yao has volunteered and participated in charity events, both in his homeland and in the United States.

Meanwhile, Yao's playing abilities have made him arguably the best big man in today's game. If Yao can shake off the injury problems that have nagged him over the past few seasons, he could potentially carve out a career that would land him in the **Basketball Hall of Fame**. Only time will tell what impact the giant from Shanghai has on the game of professional basketball.

A Sampling of Number One Picks in the NBA Draft

Being selected as the first pick in the NBA draft comes with a lot of pressure. Players selected first typically make the most money, and they are expected to play well shortly after entering the league. Here is a list of some number one selections and how they've done:

1984: Hakeem Olajuwon. Houston's last overall number one pick before Yao Ming, the Nigerian-born Olajuwon led the Rockets to back-to-back NBA Championships in 1994 and 1995. He was also named league MVP in 1994.

1987: David Robinson. His 14-year career with the San Antonio Spurs included two championships (2001 and 2003), as well as Rookie of the Year (1990) and league MVP (1995) honors. Robinson is considered one of the best big men in NBA history.

1992: Shaquille O'Neal. Drafted by the Orlando Magic, O'Neal won NBA Championships with the Los Angeles Lakers (2001, 2002, and 2003) and the Miami Heat (2006). A perennial All-Star, he was named Rookie of the Year in 1993 and NBA MVP in 2000. Many experts regard O'Neal as the most dominant center of his era.

1996: Allen Iverson. The Philadelphia 76ers drafted the point guard after his sophomore year at Georgetown University. Iverson won Rookie of Year honors in 1997 and was named league MVP in 2001. In career scoring average (almost 28 points per game), Iverson ranks third all time, behind only Michael Jordan and Wilt Chamberlain.

1998: Michael Olowokandi. With a career average of only 8.3 points per game, the seven-footer, drafted by the Los Angeles Clippers, has been somewhat of a disappointment.

2001: Kwame Brown. Selected directly out of high school by the Washington Wizards, Brown has struggled in the NBA. Playing for Washington, the Lakers, and the Memphis Grizzlies, he averaged fewer than 8 points and 6 rebounds per game in his first eight seasons as a pro.

2003: LeBron James. Drafted out of high school by the Cleveland Cavaliers, Brown quickly became one of the NBA's biggest superstars, winning Rookie of the Year honors in 2004 and leading Cleveland to the NBA Finals in 2007.

2005: Andrew Bogut. An Australian of Croatian descent, Bogut—who attended college in the United States—improved steadily throughout his first three seasons with the Milwaukee Bucks. But the seven-footer remained a long way from becoming one of the NBA's dominant centers.

(Go back to page 5.) ◀◀

The Cleveland Cavaliers selected LeBron James (above) right out of high school with the first overall pick in the 2003 NBA draft. "King James" has validated the Cavaliers' decision, winning Rookie of the Year honors in 2004 and leading his team to the NBA Finals in 2007. Other number one picks have not panned out quite so well.

Meet Team Yao

A number of people helped facilitate Yao's move to the NBA. Here is a short introduction to the key members of Team Yao:

Bill Duffy—a former NBA player and Yao's agent. Duffy, who represents more than 20 NBA players, helped negotiate Yao's contract with the Rockets.

Bill Sanders—an associate of Bill Duffy. Sanders is responsible for Yao's corporate deals and the media's access to the NBA star.

Erik Zhang—a Chinese-American who was born in Yao's hometown of Shanghai but lived in Madison, Wisconsin. Zhang met Yao because he was dating one of Yao's distant cousins, whom he later married. He speaks fluent English and Mandarin, and has a great understanding of the Chinese sports system. This knowledge greatly helped in convincing the CBA to allow Yao to come to the United States.

John Huizinga—associate dean of business at the University of Chicago. He assisted Zhang by using a class to come up with a marketing plan for Yao. Huizinga also helped negotiate Yao's contract with the Rockets.

Lu Hao—Yao's agent in China. Shortly before Yao left, the CBA passed a law requiring all players to have a China-based agent.

Colin Pine—Yao's translator. He lived with Yao and his parents during Yao's rookie season in the NBA. He helps with NBA-China relations as well.

(Go back to page 6.) ◀◀

A Portrait of the Athlete's Mother

Yao Ming's mother, Fang Fengdi, was a basketball star in her own right. Fang grew up in Shanghai, where sports officials noticed her height and athletic ability. At the age of 14, Feng was placed in an elite sports-training facility. After five years of training almost 10 hours each day, she was on the way to taking her place among China's top female basketball players.

But then Chinese society was thrown into chaos. In 1966 China's leader, Mao Zedong, launched a movement known as the **Cultural Revolution**. Mao's stated goal was to eliminate all the supposed enemies of Chinese **communism**. Tens of thousands of people were killed, and millions more were put into prison camps or removed from cities and made to work on large state-owned farms.

China's state-sponsored sports programs, including basketball, ceased. By 1969 the basketball program was brought back. Because many athletes had been thrown into prison, Fang was now one of the more experienced players. She became captain of the women's national team. In 1976 Fang, who was known for her relentless hustle and for her skills around the basket, led the Chinese team to victory in the Asian Championships.

Soon afterward, injuries became a problem for Fang. In 1977 she retired from competitive basketball at the age of 28. (Go back to page 11.) ◀◀

Shanghai

With a population of more than 18 million, Yao's Ming's hometown, Shanghai, is China's largest city. It is also the country's commercial capital and one of the world's most vibrant cities.

It wasn't always that way. Like much of China, Shanghai suffered during the chaos of the Cultural Revolution (1966–1976)—and before that, from the disastrous economic policies of Mao Zedong and the Chinese Communist Party.

By the time Yao was born in 1980, however, Mao had been dead for four years. A new Chinese leader, Deng Xiaoping, had begun to reform China's economy. Under Deng and his successors, Chinese society—which had long been closed to the world—slowly started to open up.

In the early 1990s, Shanghai entered a period of incredible growth. Investors and businesspeople from around the world flocked to the city, hoping to profit from China's increasing prosperity. The pace of development in Shanghai was staggering. Run-down neighborhoods and rice paddies were transformed, seemingly overnight, into gleaming shopping malls, office towers, and luxury hotels. In less than 20 years, more than 4,000 skyscrapers have been built— and Shanghai's boom shows no signs of slowing down. (Go back to page 12.) ◀◀

Neon signs light up this street in Shanghai. Yao Ming's hometown is China's largest city, with a population of more than 18 million. A commercial and financial center, Shanghai has seen tremendous growth over the past decades. Since the early 1990s, more than 4,000 new skyscrapers have been built in the city.

Chinese Players in the NBA

Yao was neither the first nor the last Chinese player to make it into the NBA. Here is a short look at the three others:

Yi Jianlian—Selected by the Milwaukee Bucks with the sixth overall pick in the 2007 NBA draft, Yi is a 6'11" forward. Between 2002 and 2007, he played for the Guangdong South Tigers in the CBA.

Wang Zhizhi—The 7'1" Wang was one of the most famous basketball players in China, thanks to his career with the Bayi Rockets, which dominated the early years of the CBA. In 1999 he was drafted by the Dallas Mavericks, but two years passed before he managed to join the team. In 2002 Wang decided not to return to China to train with the national team, a decision that caused much controversy in his homeland. By late 2005, after uninspiring stints with three teams, Wang was out of the NBA. He returned to China, apologized to the public, and went back to the Bayi Rockets.

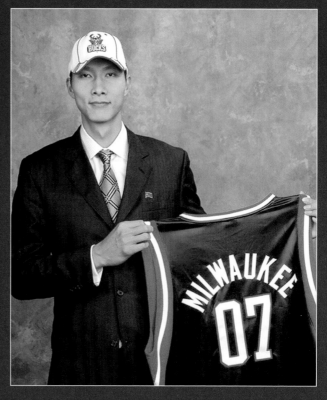

Chinese basketball star Yi Jianlian holds up the jersey of his new team, the NBA's Milwaukee Bucks, 2007. The Bucks chose the 6'11" forward from Guangdong with the sixth overall pick in the 2007 draft. In his first season in the NBA, Yi averaged a modest 8.6 points and 5.2 rebounds per game.

Mengke Bateer—The 6'11" center played for the CBA's Beijing Ducks before being invited for a tryout with the Denver Nuggets in 2001. He played 27 games for the Nuggets during the 2001–2002 season, then bounced around the NBA, leaving the league after the 2005–2006 season. Like Wang Zhizhi, he returned to his former CBA team, the Beijing Ducks.

(Go back to page 17.)

Differences Between Chinese and U.S. Basketball

There are significant differences between the Chinese Basketball Association and the National Basketball Association. Here are a few of them:

1. **Size**—The CBA is made up of 14 teams, while the NBA currently has 30 teams.

2. **Pay**—Chinese basketball players are paid according to how successful their team is. They make more money if their team wins, much less when the team loses. In the NBA, players are given a flat salary, which they are paid no matter what. Many NBA contracts do, however, include performance bonuses (if, for example, the player makes the All-Star team, or scores a certain number of points).

3. **Youth System**—In China the top basketball prospects are placed in separate schools, where the focus is on producing players for the national team through intensive training and the best available coaching. The United States doesn't have an organized national system like that. Kids learn the game on playgrounds, in youth leagues, and at school. In most cities, however, elite players have opportunities for high-level competition by the time they reach high school. Most of the best American players hone their skills on college teams.

(Go back to page 19.) ◀◀

China's national basketball team plays an exhibition game against a summer-league team sponsored by the Dallas Mavericks, at Southern Methodist University's Moody Coliseum, July 1, 2004. In China promising young players are sent to state-sponsored schools for specialized training. In the United States, kids are more likely to learn the game on playgrounds and in youth leagues.

Shaq vs. Yao: Battle of the Twin Towers

During his rookie season, Yao got a taste of playing against one of the most dominant players in the history of the game: Los Angeles Lakers center Shaquille O'Neal. Standing at 7'1" and weighing more than 350 pounds, Shaq posed quite a challenge for the taller but lighter Yao. Their two head-to-head matchups of the season received a great deal of media hype. Here is a brief recap:

January 17, 2003: In his first confrontation with the Lakers big man, Yao gave a solid performance. He scored 10 points, grabbed 10 rebounds, and blocked six shots (including two rejections of Shaq at the beginning of the game). Still, O'Neal ultimately got the better of his Chinese counterpart, dropping 31 points and pulling down 13 rebounds. The Rockets won the game, 108-104, behind 44 points from guard Steve Francis.

March 26, 2003: O'Neal dominated the game, scoring 39 points and leading his team to a 96-93 victory. Yao was limited to 6 points on 3-for-13 shooting, though he did pull down 10 rebounds.

While Shaq clearly bested Yao in these first head-to-head encounters, the two games

Shaquille O'Neal shares a word with Yao Ming before the start of a game. Shaq, widely considered the most dominant big man of his era, got the better of Yao in their first head-to-head matchups. But Shaq was in the twilight of his great career as Yao began to emerge as a superstar.

provided a clear indication that Yao Ming was in the NBA to stay. He had a long way to go, but Yao had shown flashes of brilliance against an all-time great. (Go back to page 25.) ◀◀

China Games and the NBA-China Relationship

Basketball has long been a popular sport in China. But the NBA's first visit to China came in 1979, when the Washington Bullets (now the Washington Wizards) played two exhibition games against the Chinese national team.

Since 2000 the rapid growth of the NBA in China, coupled with the emergence of Yao as one of the league's star players, has opened a brand-new market overseas. With Yao's rise to stardom, officials from the NBA and China held talks to establish exhibition games in Asia. This led to the creation of the **China Games**. These contests, played during the NBA preseason, have been staged twice. Here is a look at both China Games:

2004: With Yao as the centerpiece, the Houston Rockets traveled to Beijing and Shanghai to play against the Sacramento Kings. The Rockets and Kings each won one game apiece.

2007: The Cleveland Cavaliers and the Orlando Magic both participated in the second China Games. In all, three games were played, one in Shanghai and two in Macau. The Magic played and won all three games, beating the Cavaliers twice and the Chinese national team once.

(Go back to page 33.) ◀◀

Basketball Without Borders

A global initiative introduced by the NBA to promote the growth and development of basketball players and coaches throughout the world, Basketball Without Borders (BWB) began in July 2001. The inaugural program took place in Treviso, Italy. There, 50 promising players from the strife-torn countries of the former Yugoslavia joined Yugoslav-born Vlade Divac and Toni Kukoc as well as other former and current NBA stars for a basketball camp and tournament. The program brought expert coaching and advice to the young players. More important, it united the participants, whose countries had been at war with each other, around their mutual love of basketball.

The success of the program in 2001 led to a second event in 2002. This took place in Istanbul, Turkey, and brought together young players from Greece and Turkey. The 2003 edition returned to the original location of Treviso, Italy. That year, the **Fédération Internationale de Basketball** (FIBA) selected players from 25 countries across Europe to participate.

Encouraged by the program's success, the NBA expanded it to three continents in 2004, holding camps in Europe (Treviso), Africa (Johannesburg, South Africa), and South America (Rio de Janeiro, Brazil). The following year Asia was added, and Yao played a large role in making Shanghai the new Asian venue. Since then, BWB camps have been hosted by various cities around the world.

(Go back to page 44.) ◀◀

1980   Yao Ming is born in Shanghai, China, on September 9, 1980; he weighs over
11 pounds at birth.

1986   At six years old, Yao already stands 4 feet 10 inches tall.

1989   Touches a basketball for the first time in his life; initially doesn't like the game.

1992   Is placed in the Xu Jia Hui District Youth Sports School, a state-sponsored school for
promising young athletes.

1994   Is chosen to play for the Shanghai Sharks' youth basketball team.

1997   Makes his first appearance for the Shanghai Sharks' senior team.

1998   Visits the United States for the first time.

2000   Represents China in the Summer Olympics, held in Sydney, Australia.

2002   On April 21, wins the Chinese Basketball Association title with the Shanghai Sharks.

On June 26, is selected by the Houston Rockets with the first overall pick in the
NBA draft.

Makes his NBA debut on October 30, coming off the bench in a game against the
Indianapolis Pacers.

2003   Is the Western Conference's starting center at the NBA All-Star Game on February 9.

2004   Leads the Rockets to their first playoff appearance in five years; Houston loses in
five games to the Los Angeles Lakers in April.

2007   Marries his longtime girlfriend, Ye Li, in Shanghai on August 7.

Is named *Sports Illustrated* China Sportsman of the Year.

2008   Sustains a stress fracture that ends his season on February 26.

It is the third consecutive season in which injuries shorten his NBA season.

Awards & Honors

2003 NBA All-Star

2004 NBA All-Star

2005 NBA All-Star

2006 NBA All-Star

2007 NBA All-Star
Sports Illustrated China Sportsman of the Year

2008 NBA All-Star

NBA Stats

Regular Season	Games Played	Minutes Per Game	Rebounds Per Game	Points Per Game	Assists Per Game
2002–2003	82	29.0	8.2	13.5	1.7
2003–2004	82	32.8	9.0	17.5	1.5
2004–2005	80	30.6	8.4	18.3	0.8
2005–2006	57	34.2	10.2	22.3	1.5
2006–2007	48	33.8	9.4	25.0	2.0
2007–2008	55	37.2	10.8	22.0	2.3
Totals	404	32.5	9.2	19.0	1.6

Books

Christopher, Matt, and Glenn Stout. *On the Court with . . . Yao Ming*. New York: Little, Brown and Co., 2004.

Savage, Jeff. *Yao Ming*. Minneapolis: LernerSports, 2004.

Xiao, C. F. *Yao Ming: The Road to the NBA*. Translated by Philip Robyn. San Francisco: Long River Press. 2004.

Yao Ming, with Ric Bucher. *Yao Ming: A Life in Two Worlds*. New York: Hyperion/Miramax, 2006.

Web Sites

http://www.nba.com/playerfile/yao_ming/

Yao's player profile on NBA.com provides a short biography, news, and regular-season and playoff statistics.

http://www.yaomingmania.com/

This blog, created and maintained by a supporter of Yao, has existed ever since the big man entered the NBA.

http://www.yaomingfanclub.com/

Club Yao contains news updates, feature stories, photos, and even an occasional interview with the Chinese superstar.

http://www.nba.com/bwb/

The official Web site of the NBA's Basketball Without Borders program contains information about each year's camp locations and tournament results.

http://sports.espn.go.com/nba/players/profile?statsId=3599

Yao's ESPN player profile has links to news stories and other interesting information about the Rockets center.

agent—a person who negotiates contract terms, product endorsements, and other deals on behalf of a professional athlete.

Amateur Athletic Union—an organization dedicated to the promotion of physical fitness and nonprofessional sports competition in the United States.

Basketball Hall of Fame—a museum honoring the best all-time basketball players, located in Springfield, Massachusetts, where the game was created.

Basketball Without Borders—a global initiative, started by the NBA in 2001, that brings talented young players to basketball camps for instruction and competition.

China Games—the name given to the series of games played by NBA teams in China in 2004 and 2007.

Chinese Basketball Association—China's professional basketball league; also, the governing body that oversees China's national basketball program.

communism—a form of government characterized by state control of economic activity, supposedly for the purpose of distributing wealth fairly.

Cultural Revolution—a period in Chinese history, lasting from 1966 to 1976, during which China's leader Mao Zedong launched a violent campaign against supposed enemies of the country's Communist ideals.

culture—the pattern of human knowledge, belief, and behavior that exists in a particular geographic location.

Fédération Internationale de Basketball—the governing body of basketball for international tournaments throughout the world.

fluent—having the ability to speak a language like a native of the country.

grant—a sum of money given by an organization or government to fund a project, program, or research.

mini-camp—a short sports camp, typically lasting three or four days (often with the aim of teaching players something specific).

National Basketball Association—the premier U.S. professional basketball league, which consists of 30 teams and is considered the top basketball league in the world.

severe acute respiratory syndrome (SARS)—a contagious, flu-like illness caused by a virus; a deadly epidemic of SARS broke out in China in late 2002 and spread to several other countries before being contained by the summer of 2003.

telethon—a long television program whose goal is to raise money for a worthy cause or charity, often through appeals by celebrities.

page 6 "I want to go . . ." NBA.com, "Quotes from the Top Draft Picks," June 26, 2002. http://www.nba.com/draft2002/quotes_020626.html#yao.

page 9 "This is now a new start . . ." Ibid.

page 12 "Yao Ming, Yao Ming's parents . . ." C. F. Xiao, *Yao Ming: The Road to the NBA*, translated by Philip Robyn (San Francisco: Long River Press, 2004), 29.

page 12 "a crane towering over . . ." Craig S. Smith with Mike Wise, "Eying N.B.A., China Will Make Athletes Pay," *New York Times*, April 25, 2002. http://query.nytimes.com/gst/fullpage.html?res=9F01EEDA143EF936A15757C0A9649C8B63&sec=&spon=&pagewanted=all

page 14 "He's 7 feet 5 . . ." Robin Miller, quoted in Xiao, *Yao Ming*, p. 119.

page 17 "He is really talented . . ." Xiao, *Yao Ming*, p. 152.

page 22 "I felt especially nervous . . ." Yao Ming and Ric Bucher, *Yao Ming: A Life in Two Worlds* (New York: Miramax Books, 2006), p. 133.

page 23 "I still don't know . . ." Ibid., p. 134.

page 26 "Maybe not all NBA players . . ." Ibid., p. 132.

page 30 "The three-hour show . . ." "The Stars of Asia—Opinion Shapers: Yao Ming," *BusinessWeek* Online, June 9, 2003. http://www.businessweek.com/magazine/content/03_23/b3836626.htm

page 30 "Yao's a lot better . . ." Brett Ballantini, "Shooting Toward the Playoffs," *Basketball Digest*, January–February 2004. http://findarticles.com/p/articles/mi_m0FCJ/is_3_31/ai_112128653

page 34 "You wouldn't believe the difference . . ." Ric Bucher, "How Yao Finally Became a Dominant NBA Player," *ESPN the Magazine*, April 12, 2006. http://sports.espn.go.com/nba/columns/story?columnist=bucher_ric&id=2404746

page 37 "The final goal before . . ." Jonathan Feigen, "Rest Not at Top of Yao's 'To-Do' List This Summer," *Houston Chronicle*, May 10, 2006. http://www.chron.com/disp/story.mpl/sports/3852710.html

page 39 "He's arguably the top center . . ." Jonathan Feigen, "Yao Takes Cautious Approach to Toe Injury," *Houston Chronicle*, October 5, 2006. http://www.chron.com/disp/story.mpl/sports/4237435.html

page 42 "I didn't do my job . . ." Michael Murphy, "Yao: Blame Me for 1st Round Flameout," *Houston Chronicle*, May 6, 2007. http://www.chron.com/disp/story.mpl/sports/bk/bkn/4779281.html

page 47 "I think I need . . ." Jonathan Feigen, "Rockets Notes," *Houston Chronicle*, October 12, 2007. http://www.chron.com/disp/story.mpl/sports/bk/bkn/5208050.html

page 48 "If I cannot play . . ." Associated Press, "China's National Team Hoping Yao Will Return for Games," February 27, 2008. http://sports.espn.go.com/nba/news/story?id=3266723

Numbers in ***bold italics*** refer to captions.

Travis Clark is a freelance writer and editor.

PICTURE CREDITS

page

1: Garmin International/NMI

4: Fine Line Features/NMI

7: Jeff Balke/CIC Photos

8: Jeff Wang/CIC Photos

10: Roybin/SPCS

13: W. Peng/IOW Photos

15: Nathaniel S. Butler/NBAE/Getty Images

16: Fernado Rodriguez/NBAE/PRMS

18: T&T/IOW Photos

20: Fine Line Features/PRMS

22: Fine Line Features/PRMS

23: Philadelphia Inquirer/KRT

25: Feature China Photos

26: Atlanta Journal-Constitution/KRT

28: Bill Baptist/NBAE/Getty Images

31: Roybin/SPCS

32: NBAE/NMI

35: Issac Baldizon/NBAE/Getty Images

36: Nathaniel S. Butler/NBAE/Getty Images

38: dbmboise/IOW Photos

40: Fox/KRT

41: Bill Baptist/NBAE/Getty Images

43: Garrett W. Ellwood/NBAE/Getty Images

45: Color China Photo

46: Jesse D. Garrabrant/NBAE/Getty Images

48: McDonald's Corp./NMI

51: Sports Illustrated/NMI

53: Color China Photo

54: Jennifer Pottheiser/NBAE/SPCS

55: ChinaFotoPress

56: Jamie Squire/Getty Images

Front cover: Andrew D. Bernstein/NBAE/PRMS